The

COSMIC

ORDERING

Service

The COSMIC ORDERING *Service*

BARBEL MOHR

HAMPTON ROADS
PUBLISHING COMPANY, INC.

Translated into English
by Heike Müller, Oakland, California
Guided meditation in Chapter 6 by Prageet Peter Harris.
Used by permission of the author and Stargates.

Cover design by Marjoram Productions
Digital Imagery © copyright 2001 PhotoDisc, Inc.

For information write:

Hampton Roads Publishing Company, Inc.
1125 Stoney Ridge Road
Charlottesville, VA 22902

434-296-2772
fax: 434-296-5096
e-mail: hrpc@hrpub.com
www.hrpub.com

If you are unable to order this book from your local
bookseller, you may order directly from the publisher.
Call 1-800-766-8009, toll-free.

Library of Congress Catalog Card Number: 2001094006
ISBN 1-57174-272-7

Originally published as "Bestellungen beim Universum" by
Omega-Verlag
Karlstr. 32
D-52080 Aachen, Germany
Copyright © 1998
by Omega-Verlag
ISBN 3-930243-13-X

10 9 8 7 6 5 4 3

Printed on acid-free paper in Canada

Contents

Preface by the Author

Dear Reader,

Welcome to my little guidebook to "cosmic ordering." If, after reading this book, you think that cosmic ordering is total nonsense, but you decide to place an order with the universe anyway just to prove me wrong, then you have subscribed to this ordering service just the way I first did. And you just might start as wonderful a journey toward an easier, more fulfilling life, involving less struggle, as I did.

I once heard a lecture by Erhard Freitag during which he pointed out: "If you really know something, i.e., if you have perfected it, you will just live it without giving it a second thought. You will be a living demonstration of this knowledge. But if you are still working on gaining knowledge of something and teaching yourself about it, you may find that, one day, you will start teaching it to others."

What I am trying to say is that I have not yet perfected cosmic ordering either, but I really love practicing it every day. And in doing so, I have already come across so many miracles that I am unable to count them any more. I practice ordering a lot, but I practice without expending any effort, because if there were any effort involved whatsoever, I would have given up a long time ago. Sometimes I am quite lazy, you know, and by now, I am really spoiled by this excellent cosmic ordering service!

For me:
* it has to be easy;
* it has to be fun;
* it has to generate more energy than I put in.

The cosmic ordering service meets all these requirements. Therefore, I recommend that you try it yourself!

Have fun reading!

P. S. By the way, you don't have to have read all the chapters to start ordering. Just start whenever you feel like it, and read as much or as little as you want. This book contains many tips and helpful hints. Look for the things that interest you or catch your eye. Picking up the book every once in a while to read some more, or opening up the book to any page, is more helpful than digging your way through the book, chapter by chapter (although this is permitted if you prefer it that way). Only you know what is the most enjoyable way for you. Simply listen to your inner voice.

1

How I Discovered the "Cosmic Ordering Service"

The whole thing started a few years ago during an argument with a friend. She had read a book about positive thinking and suggested that I imagine the perfect man with all the right qualities and just ask the universe to send him my way, to "place an order" for him with the universe. Back then I was not thinking highly of those kinds of ideas, and got all worked up as the discussion progressed. I thought I needed to save my friend from pending madness. We finally ended our argument with the agreement that I would place a "test order" to prove to her what total nonsense this was. At that time, I had a nine-item wish list for the perfect man, which included: he must be a vegetarian, be against alcohol, be a non-smoker, and know T'ai Chi.

In order to minimize the statistical probability of a coincidence as much as possible, I set an exact delivery date; it would be during a specific week in approximately three months. With that, the discussion was temporarily concluded.

When said week arrived, a guy who had all nine characteristics was promptly delivered.

"Wowwww!" I thought. After that I was convinced that this cosmic ordering service was definitely worth trying and got into an ordering frenzy.

I still do everything in my daily life as well as I can in that moment, and I am surely not the passive kind who just hops into a hammock and does nothing but order. Nevertheless, whenever something comes up that I would like to have, but I cannot find a way of getting for myself, I order it: an office, money (this works for me in sums of a few thousand dollars; I have too many doubts about higher sums, which blocks the flow), job, apartment, etc.

Some time ago, I had a position in a public relations office, and part of my job involved generating an informational flyer by cutting and pasting portions from other sources. I had total freedom in the design of the flyer and enjoyed it so much that I wanted to study magazine design. I checked into taking evening classes in computer graphics—today almost all magazines are computer generated—but the classes were expensive and took years to finish. It wasn't worth this kind of effort to me. So here was an obvious case for another order, just for fun.

It couldn't hurt. And while I was at it, I added that I wanted to work in a small, comfortable place in the country, and that the director of the company should be my age, and a charming, non-choleric person . . . if you please.

Shortly thereafter, a colleague of mine quit her job. She changed positions several times during the next few months and finally ended up in a small company in the country. Her boss was a charming, twenty-six-year old, and she was doing the graphic work there all by herself. At first I was totally baffled. I order, and they deliver my order to her. Unbelievable!

At the same time I had another order in the making. An ex-friend, one whom I had not ordered, owed me quite a lot of money. I had ordered this amount returned to me, with no regard to its source. The money, therefore, would not necessarily come from him; he did not have any more money anyway.

It so happened that I also changed jobs and started working for a magazine. The magazine didn't make it, and discontinued after four months. But due to their long term-of-notice requirement, I got, approximately, the amount that I had ordered—more than twelve thousand dollars—as a settlement. Isn't that outrageous?

Suddenly blessed with that kind of money, my first thoughts were to leave the country and learn Italian. But I had to cancel these plans. The earlier order was in the delivery phase: my former colleague called and said she urgently needed help. She had convinced her boss, the twenty-six-year-old, that she needed one month to find an assistant. That, she told me, would give her enough time to train me in computer layout design.

The office was in the country. We worked at a wooden table with bench in the garden, the two of us designing six totally different technical journals, and the boss throwing erasers at us for fun. I stayed there for two years. It was great!

My favorite objects to order at that time were men. After the nine-item wish list came the improved fifteen-item list. But when that also was not accurate enough, I wanted to be prepared for any contingencies, and put together the enhanced twenty-five-item "male order" list; all quite comprehensive, even including the delivery date. This was in case the "ones on high" should take their time. But, the order had a flaw. It is amazing how many model variations there are that one doesn't take into account. Although the delivery model had all twenty-five characteristics, I had more stress with the twenty-five-item guy than I have had with some "zero-item types." The number of items is, apparently, no guarantee of anything.

Only recently, a good friend of mine came up with the glorious idea to simply order "the one that is the best match for me at this moment." Either the idea was so simple I didn't even think of it, or I lacked faith that "the ones on high" would come up with something good. This friend of mine, however, is convinced that his wording was the key, and is highly satisfied with the delivery that happened three days later.

I am afraid it's a trust issue for me. I secretly

accuse the cosmic ordering service of continuing to leisurely "play the harp" for a while longer before taking action, unless I "turn up the pressure" and specify the delivery date. And it is exactly the other way around: The more faith I have, the faster it works.

By the way, I placed my very first order very romantically, on the balcony in the moonlight. By now, however, I order from everywhere, and in any which way I please. At one time I wanted to have an inexpensive office very close to where I live, and I wanted it within the next few days. I placed that order very matter-of-factly, directly from my desk. Three days later my neighbor called me over and offered just such an office to me. You can imagine that I felt just a little shocked by this rapid delivery. In the end, I didn't take the office as the whole project for which I needed an office was still up in the air. I had ordered a little too soon.

> **REMEMBER:** Be aware of what you wish for and order; it could come true at once! Otherwise, you may get so wrapped up in placing orders that you lose track of whether the things you ordered are really good for you. It is better to pause for a moment and get in touch with your inner self before placing an order.

One of my especially dear friends always laughs so hard he almost drops the phone when I tell him about my ordering successes. His opinion is: "For those whom God wants to punish, He grants their wishes." Of course, this expression is totally outdated.

Punishment is out, mega-out. On the contrary, I find that even those orders that I throw away right after they get delivered are extremely useful because who knows how long it would have taken me, otherwise, to find out that I don't want that order? Maybe I would have pursued this or that dream for years. This way I get to the essence of what I really want in life much more quickly. But if you pause frequently and listen to your inner voice, you spare yourself many superfluous orders.

REMEMBER, TOO: You do not need to apply a special breathing technique or get into a trance to program your subconscious. You also do not need to read the order to yourself while in a headstand under hypnosis. You only need to simply say, think, and feel, as guileless as a child, what you would like to have, and it will come.

CAUTION: That of which you are secretly afraid will come first. Neither your subconscious, nor the universe, understands the expression: "I do not want this and that." Or: "I hope that in the end this and that will not happen." The words "no" and "not" are to be scratched, and then you will see the image in your mind begin to materialize. For example: Sit down quietly and do not think of a polar bear for three minutes. You probably haven't ever thought about polar bears as intensely as just then in your entire life. Therefore: Everything that you do not want and have as an image in your mind, at a minimum, blocks the true wish. "First you have to believe, then trust, and soon the proof from the universe will come. It manifests through your belief. This is the spiritual law of the universe."

One day you will know—trusting belief without doubt—that everything you wish and need comes to you anyhow. If something goes wrong, it can only mean that something even better is waiting for you, or that there is a flaw in your wish that you cannot see yet. You will know that the best is still to come and that it will, no doubt, come soon. Initially you don't even necessarily have to really believe in the process; I didn't believe it during the argument with my friend, either.

It is sufficient to be open to the possibility that it could work. You will receive help from inside of you because nature is interested in happy people, and happy people respect nature and handle it with care.

2

We Practice Cosmic Ordering

I recommend that you practice cosmic ordering by placing small and "inconsequential" orders. This way your confidence will grow, and the more confidence you have, the faster your wishes will come true.

My studio, for example, is too small for a washing machine, so I take my laundry to the nearest laundromat. Recently I discovered that dryer number 9 is the hottest and dries the fastest. Dryer number 11, however, is the most ineffective and slowest. "Okay, next time I want to get dryer number 9 right away, if you please," was my order of the day.

So, last week at the laundromat, my laundry was in the spinning cycle and I was peeking over at the dryers. "Wait a minute! Didn't I order dryer number 9? Oh well, that didn't work out, I guess. Number 9 is occupied. Instead, my 'favorite,' number 11, is available. Well, maybe number 9 will be available in a minute. It can't be that only the worst dryer is available for me." But even if that were so, I was in way too good a mood to have it spoiled by a mere dryer.

"La di da di da," I was humming to myself. The spinning cycle was coming to an end and the drum was slowing down. The second my washer signaled the end of the washing cycle, dryer number 9 stopped and a lady walked over there right away to remove her laundry. So I had received my requested number 9 at exactly the right time, to the second.

If something like this happens once a year you might argue that it was just pure coincidence. But the more open-minded you are, the more frequently you will run into these mysterious "coincidences," and in the end, things work out the way you want them on a daily basis. You don't have to struggle with life so much, no matter what you do, and this means more fun, free time, and enjoyment for *you*.

Another ordering example: As mentioned before, my studio is very small, only 360 square feet, and I live, sleep, and work there. Quite cozy. Something bigger wouldn't be so bad sometimes. Something like a nice little castle, for example. But it can't cost much, of course, because now I don't pay more than five dollars per square foot for rent, and I don't really want to pay more. Otherwise, I would have to work more; and to work more just to pay the rent is no fun whatsoever.

So, just for fun, I placed the following order with the universe: "Please send a castle!" Approximately one year after this "just-for-fun" order, which I had placed together with a friend, it just so happened that another friend of mine moved into a castle for real. After he had lived and worked there for a little while, I got to know the castle during a weekend visit, and I fell in love with it. It resembles a version of Pippi Longstocking's house for adults. There are hallways, staircases, corners, and nooks and crannies everywhere. It is big, yet comfortable.

Seeing this castle and thinking how ideal it would be to live and work as a team in such a place didn't take much effort. A few weeks later this friend of mine, the owner of the castle, called me. They needed help and maybe I could join their team; and, of course, I could also live at the castle.

I decided to visit the castle again, and promptly received three more neat stories about coincidences for my "Book of Coincidences." (I collect the best stories about coincidences anybody wants to share with me.) As it turned out, the teamwork at the castle could have only worked out as a part-time occupation for me, since I didn't have quite the right skill set for what they needed. In addition, I would have lived a little too far away from my boyfriend, which I didn't really like, either. And as beautifully enchanting as this castle is, with its chapel, and sixty-three rooms, it is really more like a citadel, lying in a hillside, with no park around it.

So, castle with park and closer to my boyfriend would really be nicer. But sharing housing and working together, that's cool! I was just thinking that to myself. And sometimes when I am just thinking to myself, I wonder if maybe there isn't someone sitting in my brain who tells me to wish for exactly the things that will happen anyway. It can't be possible that so often things happen exactly as I have wished!

You see, another friend of mine had, in the meantime, come up with another castle. It is in the process of being remodeled to house a conference center and vegetarian culinary academy. It is situated south of Munich, and closer to where my boyfriend lives. And it has a beautifully cute park, naturally, with view of a lake from the patio. Of course, this friend of mine invited me to visit the castle one Sunday morning and, of course, the manager was there, even though it was a Sunday. Of course, I liked the manager and, of course, they will need help with all kinds of things once the remodeling is done. We could get together and talk about this some more. . . .

In the meantime, I am working on the *Book of Coincidences* and publishing my own (positive) magazine, which takes up a lot of my time. That means it is questionable whether I will actually work in any castle in the future. My lax attitude toward the fulfillment of my wishes made one of my friends ask: "Aren't you afraid of the 'bill' the ordering service might send you? You go around and place orders left and right for the wildest and most Utopian things, get them delivered, nevertheless, and then don't use them. That surely isn't the proper way to behave."

"The world is what you believe it is," was the only reply I could make to her. If you think in the back of your mind, "I don't deserve this," then it won't work. And, if on top of that, you are afraid of "bills," or even "punishment," then you will create exactly *that* yourself. Because, "the world is what you believe it is!"

So, to the contrary, I have the feeling that I get an extra bonus for all the many nice orders I am placing; as if the employees of the ordering service give special promotional gifts to repeat clients who order large quantities.

So, in a mysterious way, this ordering technique has the invaluable advantage that you don't ever feel all alone any more. And this feeling gets stronger the more you use the ordering service. "Dear universe, I cannot find my glasses; please, drop a hint as to where I have left them this time. Ah, here! Thanks a lot.

"This article I'm working on for magazine such-and-such urgently needs more punch to pep it up a little. Hi, ordering service, any ideas? What? Where? Which box do I need to rummage through? But there is only garbage in that one! No, I can't believe it; it has been years now since I kept this note. Fits perfectly; it's exactly what I was looking for!"

Maybe you are only talking to yourself, with

your own subconscious. That really doesn't matter at all, as long as it works. The long-term research of Dr. Elisabeth Kübler-Ross regarding near death experiences (see chapter 11), and the experiences of some of my psychically gifted friends often make me wonder, however. One should be open to all possibilities, I think. However, I look at it more from a practical standpoint: What counts is that it works!

Anyway, coming back to my ordering of odds and ends. Sometimes we encounter crises in our lives (just a possibility). The shock and trauma make us forget everything and we don't know how to get out of this predicament, or how to help somebody . . . can you do that anyway? But, the more comfortable you feel ordering with the universe, the easier it is for you to order helpful suggestions and solutions for crisis situations. You stay calmer, too. I always have in the back of my mind: "Oh well, if I cannot accomplish it on my own, I will go ahead and order it, even if it's only a useful idea that I order."

I realize that subconsciously I have probably ordered this crisis or that for myself, as well. Everything that contributed to the crisis was first inside of me. But isn't it nice to know that at least you can consciously order a good solution in case you have a total blackout? From "victim to victor" is my motto. In my opinion, a "sharp" person isn't necessarily one who knows everything and for whom everything always works out; instead, it is a person who can observe him- or herself and make conscious decisions in every situation. What do I want to think, and what do I want to create through my thoughts and emotions? Clear intentions—orders—lead to clear deliveries. And as you have seen before, even castles and many other unlikely wishes are accessible through the cosmic ordering service's vast supply catalog!

Following are a few chapters with helpful hints and suggestions about how to more easily get into the "flow of things," and be more open to and trusting in the process: a type of ordering training, so-to-say. It is actually not quite so easy, you know. On the contrary, it is terribly difficult. But there is only one real difficulty: To comprehend with body and soul how simple the process is. There is often a programmed voice inside of us that repeatedly tells us that life is difficult. Comprehend that it is simple and it will immediately become easy!

3

Test: Will the Cosmic Ordering Service Work for Me?

This test is very simple. Sit down and think about what kinds of people you met during the week, or in the course of last week if today is Monday. People in the office, on the streets, in cafés, your friends; how were they? Were they in a good mood? Competent? Incompetent? Were they all nice? All "assholes"? All unfriendly, driving like idiots? "Nope, they always let me merge right away."

Go through the entire week before you read on!

Okay. Have you gone through the entire week? Then here comes the do-it-yourself analysis: According to the law of resonance, you can only attract the kinds of people and situations from out-side of yourself that mirror your inner self. If you can see the beauty in the other person, then you have just discovered the beauty of your inner self. If everybody is giving you a hard time, then in fact you are, really, giving yourself a hard time.

This small parable will explain the concept:

The Hall of One Thousand Mirrors

Somewhere, in a land far away, there was a temple that housed a hall of one thousand mirrors. One day it so happened that a dog got lost in the temple and arrived at this hall. Suddenly confronted with one thousand of his mirror images, he growled and barked at these presumed enemies. These, however, returned his growling and teeth flashing a thousand times over. The dog in turn got even more aggressive. And as the situation got more and more heated, the dog got more and more out of control, and finally reached such an extreme state of aggression and exertion that he dropped dead.

Some time passed, and along came another dog, who also got lost in the temple and arrived at the same hall of one thousand mirrors. This dog, too, saw that he was surrounded by one thousand dogs of his kind. He then started to wag his tail with joy at these other dogs and, in return, one thousand dogs happily wagged their tails back at him. Happy and encouraged, the dog found a way out of the temple.

Nobody will ever find out, but ask yourself: Are

you more likely to behave like the first dog, or the second one? "Number 2" dogs will most definitely be better at using the cosmic ordering service.

If you are a "dog number 1 type," you should consider using the cosmic ordering service even more so. Nature is interested in happy people because they take better care of the planet and all its inhabitants, plants, and animals. And happy people want to share their inner abundance of joy, and care for and protect nature.

So, all "number 1 dogs" are encouraged to open up to the possibility that one can receive a helpful nudge from somewhere—most likely from a place which one would least expect—and that the cosmic ordering service will work increasingly better the more it is used.

4

Why Does This Technique Work?

Everything Is Living and All Is One

In 1987, researchers for the first time put a computer's CPU under extreme stress by giving it a huge number of calculations to make. One line of the programming instruction code read (in computer language of course): "If you find a solution for the following problem you may stop working." The solution was not put into the program, but nevertheless the computer found it, even faster each time it was switched on and off again. In fact this now works on every PC by means of the appropriate software. (There is more about this at www.raum-energie-forschung.de.)

Scientists are confronted by mysterious phenomena every now and again, but they have yet to come up with an explanation for why some things work. The problem is that the laws of science only work within a specified, closed system. But in reality, there is no such thing as a closed system. We are always surrounded and influenced by the energies of the entire universe. Once scientists begin to reach an understanding of this reality, they will be able to understand and explain today's "miracles."

Bending Spoons with the Power of the Mind . . .

It isn't matter that is at the core of reality; it is the vibration of matter that forms our reality. This view is supported by recent findings in physics, especially quantum physics. If, after all, the core of an atom were the size of a pea, the electrons would circle that core at a distance of approximately 500 feet, and the remaining space would be made up of no-thing-ness and energy. And even the atomic core and electrons are, in the end, nothing but tiny light particles, which essentially are just pure vibrations. In other words, you can search as much as you want, but there is no such thing as solid matter anywhere.

For example, I always thought that Uri Geller, the spoon bender, was just an accomplished illusion artist who was doing his tricks really well. But I have been "corrected" by several of my friends and acquaintances. Bending spoons? No problema. As a matter of fact, the spoon consists mostly of no-thing. The fact that the spoon "ordinarily" keeps the shape of a spoon is due to its conscious awareness of this shape. The real miracle isn't the fact that you can soften and modify the spoon with your mind power, given the 500 feet of space between the atomic core and the electrons; the miracle is that this no-thing-ness is able to stay in a stable shape at all. A real puzzle!

My friend Reiner, for example, talks to the spoon and takes it seriously, because it is part of the universal consciousness. He tells the spoon that it can stand out from the remaining one hundred thousand spoons as a very special piece of art, if it allows itself to become soft and bendable. He strokes the spoon and "schmoozes" it. Within a second, he twists the spoon several times to form a spiral, maybe with an additional bend to the front, the side, or the back, whatever comes up. Afterwards, the spoon looks like it had been melted and then totally twisted around. Without prior "permission" of the spoon, you can only get the same results with a pair of pliers and a furnace. But if you talk nicely to the spoon . . .

Another friend of mine sends energy from the sun into the spoon, and yet another acquaintance asks her guardian angels for help. The method doesn't seem to matter much; what counts is your trust that it will work.

In short: If one can twist super strong stainless steel spoons into spirals just like that, then one should also be able to simply order the right apartment, the right partner, the ideal job, etc., from the universe!

REMEMBER: Thoughts create matter. And if you need a physical demonstration, either order one from the universe, or attend a spoon-bending seminar or something similar.

"Free Energy" . . .

. . . is a concept Indian Yogis have been aware of for some time. They summon the power of free energy through dancing rituals or breathing techniques, and are then able to conquer pain. After such a preparatory ritual, a dozen spears are driven into their skin, for example, and not one drop of blood gets spilled, and no wounds or scars form. It gets especially interesting when one of the yogi masters then decides to really show off. There is one who cuts off a piece of his tongue in front of a Western audience, with cameras running; then he shows the cut-off piece and the "tongue remainder" around the circle and waits until the camera gets a close-up shot. Then he "pastes" the cut-off piece seamlessly back into place. Only one thing is absolutely prohibited: no skeptic is allowed to touch him during this performance. If you have ever experienced different vibrational frequencies and energies yourself, you already know why: The lower frequency vibrations from a tense, skeptic person can lower the master's vibrations in such a way that he will be unable to properly paste his tongue back together.

It's the same thing as if you were going to the office in an exceptionally good mood, singing and whistling, and right away somebody gets into your face: "Oh, good God, how horrible! Are you trying to kill us with that whistling of yours? Cut it out!" Your mood immediately hits rock bottom and you can't get the melody back together any more. In the same way, this yogi master cannot get his tongue back together any more.

7:10,000

With our left, logical side of the brain, we can take in approximately seven impressions per second (light, sounds, smells, etc.). With the right, creative side of the brain we can process up to 10,000 impressions per second. Most of these then get stored in our subconscious. In other words: The ratio of things we can consciously see and understand, to things our inner voice, our subconscious, knows, is approximately 7:10,000. In this sense, we know at least one thousand times as much as we know that we know. Got that?

5

How Does the Cosmic Ordering Service Work, and Why Do I Need to Be in a Good Mood to Do It?

First, a short example: Magdalene Ertl lives on the third floor of an apartment complex and parks her car in the parking garage below the building on a regular basis. One day, she wanted to take the elevator down to the parking garage, as usual, to get to her car. But then she had this sudden inclination to take the stairs instead. And without giving it another thought, she was going down the stairs.

When she passed the first floor, she saw that a courier was headed toward the front door to deliver a package. Suddenly she knew why she had come down the stairs. She opened the door to greet the surprised courier and said: "I know whose package this is; it's for me." And she was right.

Great things sometimes become obvious in small events.

Of course, the courier would have come back the next day. But who knows how often we zoom by unique opportunities via elevator because we disregard the small impulses. "Why stairs? I always take the elevator."

And that's exactly how it works with the cosmic ordering service, too. You place your order, and the UPS (Universal Parcel Service) follows you around to deliver the order. But you, stubborn as usual, won't listen to your gut feelings. "Why stairs? I always take the elevator."

As in real life, the Universal Parcel Service will try to deliver the order again and again; they want to get rid of these parcels, too, you know. The more open you are, the more you trust, and the more you are who you are, the easier it will be for you to access and listen to your inner voice and to disregard what others may think of you. Your most important questions are: What are my gut feelings? Do I really want this? Is that really *me*? Do I want to lounge on the sofa tonight instead of going to this terribly important dinner with these people? And even if I decide to go, can I be consciously happy about the fact that I *decided* to go when I don't *have to* do anything?

With this in mind, you will become more sensitive, and when you get a call from the "cosmic ordering service" to your gut, you'll *follow it*. For example, your gut may say something like this:

Barbel Mohr

"Get up an hour early today and go jogging." Or, "Take the stairs." Or, "Please, head around the block to the left first this time and talk to the old man at the kiosk. He has a nice nephew who works at a company where your dream job will become available soon, but we won't tell you about that until three months from now."

6

How Do I Learn to Listen to My Inner Voice?

(So I Won't Miss Where and When My Order Is Going to Be Delivered)

So now have we arrived at the most difficult chapter? No. Fooled you! This is really the easiest chapter.

The technique is extremely simple, but in order to explain why it works so well and why this point is so important, I have to go back a few steps.

It has to do with *making a stronger commitment to yourself.*

What is that supposed to mean? It simply means that in making a stronger commitment to yourself, you make it very clear to yourself and your subconscious that you want to live your truth. Just a reminder: nature is interested in happy people, because happy people care about nature. Newborn babies, for example, aren't in a bad mood or trying to be cool. Researchers have shown that autogenic training (meditation focused on removing tension in the body and promoting deep breathing) and deep relaxation change the surface tension of the skin. And it is impossible to have negative thoughts when in a totally relaxed state.

It is impossible to have negative thoughts when in a relaxed state.

That means your natural state is happiness. In order to be unhappy, you have to be tense and uptight. If you make a stronger commitment to yourself, you also make it clear that you will use all the courage it takes to live your truth. You make it clear that you want to live in unity and in love and in the joy that naturally follow all these things.

Following is the written version of a guided meditation (reprinted with permission of the author and Stargates). The meditation participants lie on blankets on the floor, relax to soothing, meditative music, and listen to the following words. Although you have to read the words yourself, they will be just as meaningful, and this shouldn't keep you from making your favorite tea, however, and listening to some nice music, if you wish.

Make a Stronger Commitment to Yourself

Do you want to move out of your old, restrictive habit patterns quickly? Do you want to get rid of automatic behaviors and those habits that are no longer serving you? It is very easy. All you need is to make a stronger commitment to yourself.

In the past, these behaviors and patterns were of benefit to you, but their usefulness is long gone. These patterns were created in your early childhood or perhaps carried through many of your past lives. You are all carrying so many automatic unconscious patterns or behavior paths that, in truth, are no longer you. But they are still there; they are still affecting you, because they have moved into your unconscious. And so it is, by the very nature of your unconsciousness, something that you are not aware of. And so you are controlled in a sense by this habit pattern, by these thought forms that, if you were aware of them, you would choose not to have. Some of them you are aware of. You would prefer not to have them and yet you somehow continue to re-live this automatic action, time and time again. It is time to let these things go. They are in your way. Anything that is automatic is a hindrance to you.

Life has to become a path of increasing awareness, and so we suggest that you start making a stronger commitment to yourself. It is very simple. It is very, very simple. All that is needed is the intention to become free and, with this intention, to ask yourself to make a stronger commitment to yourself. So what does this mean, this stronger commitment to yourself? What is it? How does it affect you?

What is it for? Allow the words to move through you, while you read them. Try not so much to think or, at least, don't just *think* about them. The meaning will also go in without your thought processes.

When you make a stronger commitment to yourself, you are making a declaration to yourself and to the whole of existence. You are declaring your intention to live your truth. You are declaring your intention to claim the courage required to live your truth. You are declaring that you wish to live in oneness, and in love, and in the joy that naturally follow these things. Each time you are making a stronger commitment to yourself, you are stating all these things in this simple phrase: "I make a stronger commitment to my-self."

You have been taught something very different. You have been taught to take care of others first. You have been told: First you have to take care of the wife or the husband or the beautiful children. You have to take care of the parents and the grandparents. You have to take care of your friends and your neighbors, and you have to do all of these things before you take care of yourself.

Society teaches you to sacrifice, to put others first.

Dear reader, this is a way of keeping you out of your own power; keeping you disconnected from your own source. Make a stronger commitment to yourself. Put yourself first. Before all others, take care of yourself. Before the wife or the husband, before the beautiful children, before your parents. Put yourself first. Take care of yourself. Live your own truth and things will start changing in your life.

When you put others first, when you are

working to take care of others before yourself, you become tired, you become drained. You do not want to do another thing. And when you are feeling this tiredness, this exhaustion, and you have to do yet another thing, resentment happens. You become resentful that you have to take care of these others while you are so tired. You become resentful that you do not have time for yourself. But you have already been programmed to think that this is what you should do and so, of course, you do not express this resentment. So you keep it inside and the resentment grows into anger and frustration.

And because you are feeling angry and frustrated and you know that you should be helping others and not feeling bad or guilty, you start judging yourself: "I am not good enough. I can not take care of all these things which I have to take care of before my-self. I am not good enough. I am not strong enough. I should be loving these people and I am hating them."

The self-judgment grows. The anger and frustration with the others grow. But, of course, you keep it all inside. And the joy of helping others disappears, drowned in this anger, and this frustration, and this self-judgment. Dear reader, make a stronger commitment to yourself.

Put yourself first. Take care of yourself. When you love yourself, there is great joy inside. When you are loving yourself, when you are feeling joyful, you are looking around and asking: "How can I share my joy? How can I share this love? This love is so much, who can take it? Whom can I share it with?" For there is so much more inside wanting to come out. And then you start helping others, but with joy and with great appreciation, for they are allowing you to share some of this love, some of this joy. You really appreciate the opportunity. Giving from this place of abundance brings great joy. Always put yourself first and make a stronger commitment to yourself.

Consider the husband or father who has to go to work every day because he has to take care of the family; he wants to take care of the family, he loves them. But because he does not allow himself to take care of him-self first, resentment creeps in. He has to go to work because he needs the money to pay the bills. Because he has to go to work, he has to do what the boss says, even if it is not his truth. If the boss says do it, he has to do it.

Because, if he speaks his truth, he may no longer have a job and so, instead of living his truth, he says: "Yes, Sir; of course, sir. Three bags full, Sir." He gives his power away. He no longer lives his truth because he is afraid of losing his job and of not being able to take care of the family. And so he works in a job where he does not feel the joy of living his truth. He feels resentful toward the boss for telling him to do things that he does not wish to do. Or, he does not like the way the boss treats him, but he has to take care of the family and so he has to suffer: No energy; no joy; no living his truth.

He goes home, tired, frustrated, shut down. Because he has to shut down his feelings and his expressions at work every day, it becomes a habit. He remains shut down when he returns home. His family is waiting for him and wanting to share their joy, but all he can do is sit and look at the television or read the newspaper. He has very little to say . . . shut down from his feelings. And the resentment grows. It is resentment toward his family because they are keeping him in this job. He has to do this because of them. The love that is there for the wife and the beautiful children gets drowned in resentment, in anger, in frustration.

This is your world. The stories may be a little different from case to case, but this is your world. Make a stronger commitment to yourself!

When you make a stronger commitment to yourself, there is joy. You feel connected to yourself, you feel connected to the universe. If you go to work and the boss is unreasonable and will not discuss the issue with you, you will not wish to stay there. You will simply leave. You will no longer do a job simply for the money. And you will not be afraid. Because you are feeling your connection to yourself, you are feeling your connection to the whole universe. You know that as you speak your truth, you will be supported. As you live your truth, you will be supported. You feel it. You know it.

And so you simply move away and take another job where you can be honored, where you can be creative, where you can go home filled with joy from a day of creation and sharing with friends. You will take this joy home to the family. And you will have great respect and love for them. And the love that drew the husband and wife together, the love that drew the children to be with them, grows, becomes deeper, and touches many. Dear reader, it is time. It is time to change. It is time to make a stronger commitment to yourself.

You are aware that you have many habits, many unconscious thought forms. You do not wish them to be there, but they are there. In the past you have tried to understand, to analyze: "Why am I like this? What have I done wrong? How can I fix it? Which therapist can I go to? How many groups can I do this year?"

You have done this. You understand a little about how these habits and thought forms have come about. We say to you now: "There is no longer time to keep on analyzing and working it out. It is time, simply, to dissolve those thought forms, those habits that are no longer serving you. This technique, this simple method is all that is needed. Simply by making a stronger commitment to yourself. That is all that is needed."

By making a stronger commitment to yourself, you dissolve those thought forms. Those thought forms are simply energy. They are held in your energy bodies because you continue to pass energy through them. Every time you think about your difficulty, your automatic habit, you are strengthening it because you are focusing upon it. Every time you try to analyze it, you are strengthening it.

So from now on, from this moment on, when you notice something about yourself that you no longer wish to have, immediately, in that moment of awareness, make a stronger commitment to yourself. These simple words, "I make a stronger commitment to my-self," are all that are needed.

In this moment of awareness, the strength and the intention of this commitment gather energy which begins to dissolve that thought form, that habit pattern. Continue to do this every time you see something that you no longer wish to have in your energy field.

And magic will happen. Be ready for the magic. Do not analyze; simply make a stronger commitment to yourself. It will take a few days of using this technique intensely, and you will begin to notice small changes. Acknowledge the changes. It is important to acknowledge the changes. You will find that you become more aware of those things that you no longer wish to have. Acknowledge that awareness, and make a stronger commitment to yourself.

These thought forms, these habit patterns will begin to dissolve. Each time, each and every time you notice something about yourself that you no longer wish to have there, do not analyze; do not try to change. Simply make a stronger commitment to yourself. This means your joy, your truth, the courage to live your truth, your love to live yourself and to be supported by the whole of existence. Tell existence you are ready to be supported; you are ready to live your truth; you are ready to live that which you are.

You are ready to make a stronger commitment to yourself. Knowing that when you are in joy, your joy overflows. This is true service. Overflowing. Existence is overflowing love, joy, and awareness. Whether your unconscious behavior is from something you learned as a child or whether it is from something from past lives, whether it is because of some implanted mechanism in your energy field, whether it is because of others connecting to you by some unseen part, however this unconscious, unwanted behavior has come about, by making a stronger commitment to yourself, it will dissolve.

Make that commitment. Hold that intention strong in your heart and allow all of existence to support you. It is time to live your truth. It is time to be yourself.

Make a stronger commitment to yourself. It is simple. It is easy. Allow it to be. Allow yourself to be.

7

In Your Natural State, You Are Relaxed

Imagine taking your shirt or sweater, the one you are currently wearing, and twisting it, pretending to squeeze out excess laundry water. In order to keep the sweater in this twisted position, you have to exert energy. As soon as you relax and let go, the fabric naturally untwists and returns to its relaxed state.

In your naturally relaxed state, it is impossible to have negative thoughts (as described at the beginning of chapter 4). You have to exert energy to be stressed and uptight.

Hello? Do you get it? You just have to do nothing and everything will fall into place. That's the entire truth . . . almost. We all have gotten quite used to being stressed and uptight! So anything that will help you relax will get you closer to your natural state of happiness and into the orientation of "I came, ordered (made a wish), and received." According to the concept of "Make a stronger commitment to yourself," you are the best person to determine what things will help you relax the most.

The following is a list of suggestions for activities that might help you relax:

1. Working out, swimming, bicycling, dancing, hiking, etc.;

2. Taking yoga classes. (Introductory classes are offered almost everywhere now);

3. Taking tai chi classes. Tai chi works with the energy flow in your body, connects the mind, body, and soul, and enhances your sensual perceptions;

4. Starting any kind of meditation practice. Whatever works for you is the "right thing";

5. Picking up an alternative medicine magazine and figuring out what cutting-edge practice would be most exciting for you. Perhaps a water-shiatsu session, maybe, or a special kind of massage;

6. Maybe the most relaxing thing for you is to unhook the phone, cook your favorite meal, and then kick back and listen to your favorite music with eyes closed;

7. Maybe you feel like taking a weekend trip

with an old childhood friend without partners. This is not meant as an act against your partner, but as an act for relaxation;

8. Sometimes it is especially beneficial to do "something radically different." Every time you do something new, you engage all your senses, and can become completely immersed and distracted from the worries of everyday life. Look for something you have never done before. Get into it particularly for that reason, and consciously enjoy every minute of this special experience. Check in with yourself later to see how you felt. Were you relaxed? Did you have fun? Or were you more stressed than usual? Select a particularly special activity, one that may bring out your childlike playfulness or your urge for troublemaking (obviously only harmless troublemaking is allowed). For example: Were you ever *(a)* in a fitness center? Why don't you try it out some time? Test the most outrageous machines. *(b)* In a Roman steam bath? *(c)* In the park, or at the supermarket at 6 A.M.? *(d)* In a bar for losers at 4 A.M.? If you don't want to stay up that late, go to bed early and get up at 3:30 A.M. to start your adventure.

Make a date with yourself. "Sure, some other time" doesn't count. Make a stronger commitment to yourself; make a date to spend some time with *you* now, and be committed to keeping it.

9. A gift to the child within you has a similarly relaxing effect. You can never be too grown-up to lose all interest in being playful. Why don't you go to an especially large toy store and buy

something for yourself (you don't have to tell the sales person that it's for you). Playing like a child puts you in a different reality, and you can forget all your tension. Maybe the thing that relaxes you the most is to read a fairy tale or your favorite children's book from way back when. Maybe you really like trying out a different look. Children like trying on new looks and costumes. How does the world react to you when you dress like a Punk? If you live in the country, you could spend a weekend in the city, go to a fine restaurant or casino, and dress in an outrageous way that you wouldn't otherwise dream of wanting to be seen in, particularly in public. Maybe it will be so much fun for you that you will still be talking about it to your grandchildren and friends twenty years from now. Maybe you even feel daring enough to visit your local rowdies' bar wearing blue-collar work clothes.

10. Infinity. You can fill in the rest yourself. Take your time. Bring your attention to how you feel in order to find the activities that would be most relaxing for you. It could change from week to week. You don't have to do the same things for relaxation over and over again. Explore what will work now, here, and today.

The more you loosen up and the more often you feel relaxed, the more you will return to your natural, stress-free state. In this relaxed state you are unable to have negative thoughts; this will make it easier for you to draw things toward you that you really want, and you will be able to order from the universe with relaxed assurance.

8

Inner Peace:
A Comprehensive Remedy

Inner peace is the one-in-a-million super-multiplier for enhancing the effectiveness of the ordering service. The reason is simple: if you have inner peace, you are more in touch with your inner voice and with the flow of energy in your body.

It all started when my Aunt Martha visited her doctor to show him all the little discomforts that had befallen her. But nowadays you can't even count on doctors to listen to your complaints any more. This doctor didn't want to see anything; these maladies were completely irrelevant to him. In his opinion, what was really relevant was how my aunt had acquired all these dis-eases. According to the doctor, the only thing in need of curing was her mental attitude. Because, when a person's soul is healthy, those little maladies disappear. It didn't take very long for the "consultation" to arrive at a discussion of the "Source of Life," love. Martha was supposed to love herself, and everyone else as well. Hard to tell which would be more difficult for her. "You just can't love everyone, as impossible as some people are, and especially the Joneses from next door," she thought.

"Yes, you can! If you were trapped in an elevator with your worst enemy for an entire day, and he told you his entire life story, then you could love even him," according to the doctor.

And then the "peace be with you" epidemic started! Whenever Martha had to deal with someone whom she, at that very moment, heartily disliked, who was getting on her nerves or was seriously upsetting her, she was supposed to think, "Peace be with you!" That was supposed to loosen up tension, smooth aggression, and calm anger, and she would get healthier by the day.

Giving it a shot doesn't hurt. The next opportunity for trying out this new "treatment" presented itself at the seafood corner in the supermarket: "Shrimp, please. No, no (peace be with you) those are prawns. (peace be with you.) No, those aren't (peace be with you) shrimp, either. Look, over there, the small ones (peace be with you)."

Finally the lady behind the counter found the right ones. A small scoop of shrimp made its way into the container and onto the scale. ("Ridiculously minuscule quantity, but I won't say anything any more. Peace be with you!"). Weighing and attaching the price label to the container—a look to the right, then to the left—the lid comes off again and the container gets filled to the top. Then the lady said with a cunning smile: "I added a little more for you." Martha was shocked. The lady couldn't have possibly noticed something, could she? But this can't really be happening!

The new "treatment" was put to the test again over the next few days, and it turned out that apparently everything is possible!

Soon after the supermarket incident, Martha's ten-year-old daughter returned home from school, wailing, "Kevin is always teasing me." Having adopted this new perspective on life, Martha immediately thought of the "peace be with you" treatment for her daughter's problem. The best thing for her daughter was for her to not get worked up and upset with Kevin, and not to feel offended. So Martha explained the "peace be with you" treatment to her daughter. Three days later: "Well, Mom, I have told Kevin, 'Peace be with you,' now a million times, but he is still such an idiot." Hmm, difficult. Maybe for some people it takes a little longer.

Not too long afterwards: "Well, Mom, you know what? Now I have told Kevin that he is an idiot and that I always think, 'Peace be with you' when he is an idiot. And now he tells Peter, 'Peace be with you,' because he thinks that Peter is such an idiot; and Lori tells Tom, 'Peace be with you' . . . !"

One should *never* underestimate the concepts children can grasp. Valentine knew perfectly well what her mother Martha was talking about. Another example out of the mouths of babes: "It is really a bummer that Grandma always thinks so negatively. She always expects the worst and then doesn't want to see anything else. We really should tell her that, don't you think?"

When we are talking "pure life," there are no differences between age groups or professions. On that level, one soul simply interacts with another and there is a level of deep understanding between them. Anyone can test the apparently coincidental similarities in experiences in the two stories for themselves. A few "Peace be with you"s down the line and you probably will have figured out for yourself how your thoughts are affecting you.

PEACE BE WITH YOU!
✳

Peace Be With You

Live from Everyday Life (I)

The bum on the escalator: Monday morning. Subway. I am on the escalator, the bum in front of me. He has just retrieved a pack of cigarettes from the garbage. Now he is opening it and realizes that no one has forgotten to finish up the last butts. "Pffft," and the empty pack flies high into the air in a wide arc and lands in front of him on the escalator.

"Scavenger, bum, looser, derelict, pessimist. No wonder society is falling apart and going to ruin!" I think.

"Well, well, now," the spiritually trained part of my consciousness steps in. "Who would want to explode so readily now?"

I have actually read and learned quite a bit in my life, and some of it I can now recall: "If people do something stupid, they do it because they presently cannot think of anything better to do." "Happy, content people honor and respect nature." "If you love someone the way he is, then his soul is happy and can heal."

Okay, okay. That's enough! I have calmed down again and think: "Peace be with you, brother." I can really feel how peace settles back into my soul. And right at the moment when I feel peace like a wave washing over me, the homeless person in front of me turns his head, looks at the cigarette pack, picks it up, and throws it into the garbage can at the top of the escalator.

Live from Everyday Life (II)

On the way to the airport: I sit in the subway one morning at 6:00 A.M., on my way to the airport, in a so-so mood. Staying in bed would have somehow been better.

Soon thereafter, an "I-thought-was-outdated-but-I-must-have-been-wrong" yuppie boards the subway and sits down diagonally in front of me. He arranges himself on his seat in a stereotypically yuppie way. Cool posture, eyebrows positioned in a way that says, "I am a slightly stressed but terribly important manager"; one hand rests on his waist, the other, indicating extreme concentration, at the forehead. Naturally, the little briefcase and cell phone are standing by; the little suit and yuppie coat, just perfect. Overall, just awful. With increasing disgust I study his arrogant and uniquely dumb facial expression.

Then it is calling me again, my spiritual consciousness: "Hey, you, you could also love that one; after spending eight hours with him in the elevator." Oh, sh . . . ! All right, I remember. But how in the world am I supposed to not let someone like him get on my nerves? That is simply impossible. Well, my friends (the ones on high, the universe, whoever), if you think I am supposed to accept *him* the way he is, then I need a little help. That is too much to ask!

I really put some effort into this monumental task and repeated "Peace be with you" over and over; "Peace be with you, you idiot." Umm . . . say again: "Peace be with you, arrogant bozo." Shit! I cannot get rid of this feeling of disgust. And the goal is to look at him without feeling disgusted.

But as usual, any time you ask for help you get it, as long as you listen to your inner voice and follow your intuition. I am lucky. A helpful idea suddenly pops into my head. I could imagine I am sitting in a movie theater and the guy has just stepped into a scene in the movie to portray an enigmatic remnant of the 1990s, à la Carroll O'Connor's Archie Bunker, always grumpy and disgusting, but always funny, too.

I don't have to look at the scene for very long; from this new perspective, this guy is awesome. Ready for an Oscar! Hollywood at its best, especially the refinement in the details: every expression, every movement from head to toe is authentic—a uniquely talented actor, even better than Robert de Niro. My feelings of disgust for him have vanished and are turning into ones of delight. I have hardly ever seen anything so cleverly comical. I am feeling better again, and the guy receives only light and clear energy from me now, not the hostile, grey, sticky energy from before. "Peace be with him!"

Live from Everyday Life (III)

Hallelujah! Well, I live in an exclusive neighborhood with entrancing ambience and exceptional neighbors. One of these exceptional neighbors—she lives in the front part of the house next door and diagonally across the courtyard—has the charming habit of using all her vocal cords with fierce power,

at 1:00 or 2:00 A.M., to shout across the courtyard:
"You bastards! You sons-of-bitches! I will sue you
all. I will show you. Bastards, traitors . . ."

She goes on and on. I don't intend to remember
every little detail of what she says, but it is
extremely uncomfortable, especially at one in the
morning. One humid summer night recently, it happened again. She was having one of her fits and
yelling and screaming at the top of her lungs.
Nobody had his window shut on a balmy night like
that and, one by one, voices from other windows
around the courtyard started yelling back at her.

"Quiet, you dumb old cow!"

"You are dumb yourself, you bastards!"

"Shut up now, would you?"

"Pipe down!"

It was quite a circus. I didn't think that it
would be very effective to join in the yelling con-
test, but on the other hand, I was dying to go to
sleep, right there and then! I started sending light
and love into the courtyard, "Peace be with you,"
and whatever else came to mind. But maybe I
wasn't focused enough or I wasn't really convinced
that the "peace be with you" treatment would be
effective in this specific situation. At any rate, the
yelling continued.

Then I started transmitting mental SOS signals
again: "Hey, my friends up high, I want to go to
sleep. Do something!" I am still not quite sure
whether there really are guardian angels or any
kind of gods or goddesses, but experience has
shown us over and over: Asking for help always
works. And it can't hurt, anyway.

I have no idea where this helpful thought came from, but I suddenly remembered one of my CDs, with chanted mantras. One of the mantras has a beautiful melody and a heavenly choir of angel-like voices singing "Hallelujah!" over and over again. Ha, I thought, I will put together a nice little surprise for all of you out there! Screaming "Quiet" won't help, but I am curious about what you are going to think about this. Turning the speaker toward the window, I loaded the CD into the stereo. At the right track, I turned up the volume to maximum blast. Three "Hallelujahs" reverberated across the courtyard (and could probably be felt for several miles around us).

I turned the volume down all the way, and listened into the night. "They are in shock now, of course," I thought to myself. "But at least our swearing Grandma over there will come back with an ironic comment." Nothing! Nothing happened, not even a peep. It was absolutely dead quiet. I could hardly believe it. I could finally go to sleep for not a peep was uttered by anybody. It doesn't matter whether it was due to the shock or to whatever else. What counts is that silence ensued. The idea had worked.

9

All Theory Is Grey—
What Counts Is the Experience!

It is fine and important to read about things and to understand them intellectually, but what counts is applying that new knowledge. It's great when you can just go ahead and do so. That is, change your life from one moment to the next. But most of us need to get a substantial, motivational kick in the butt to get started.

Some people attend seminars for that reason. There you experience "it" live and in color. What for one person is the "absolutely, not-to-be topped, unbeatable experience and total breakthrough workshop" is but a looming threat of addiction for the next person. In addition, there probably are many strange things out there in the field of self-improvement workshops. Extensive archeological digging expeditions into one's childhood are not my way of approaching this. Energy follows your thoughts and magnifies that to which we pay attention. In general, you need only to apply what was said in the chapter entitled, "How do I learn to listen to my inner voice?" For people who have difficulties getting motivated on their own and need to be kicked to get into gear, read the following account of how things may work at a workshop.

Learn About How to Think Positively in a Workshop
(An account by a participant of her experiences during her first workshop)

Who knows what to expect? I had no idea. Nevertheless, I drove over there at the time because of inner restlessness, feelings of stress, and nervous indigestion. I imagined that I would learn a variety of relaxation techniques such as autogenic training and autosuggestion, be guided through trance journeys, and listen to a little theory.

Equipped with these techniques I would go home and be able to create a state of peacefulness and relaxation whenever I needed it and thereby harmonize the psychological components of my discomforts. No question, that's exactly what I learned. But if you thought that that was all, you grossly underestimate Ms. Gudrun Freitag, who has led these kinds of seminars for fifteen years. The content of these seminars is, in part, based on the work and theory of Dr. Joseph Murphy, one of the best-known authors in the field of positive thinking.

So, ignorant as I was, I went to a four-day seminar at the Heissenhof, which is beautifully situated near Inzell in South Germany. At 2:00 P.M., the seminar commenced. Approximately fifty participants wearing loose clothing were seated on pillows and blankets on the floor, and listened to the welcoming words of the instructor and the ensuing hour of lecture. Everything was just as I had expected. But that was soon to change. The next agenda item was a big surprise.

There was a round of disco dancing to loosen up and leave all your everyday-life stresses behind, to feel more at home. And fifty people between the ages of twenty and seventy-five danced along, everyone in their own style; some with full force and energy, some shyly looking around, and a few old-timers, after cautiously surveying the room and ensuring that everything was allowed, were merrily interlocking arms and rhythmically swaying from side to side. Then we had a coffee break.

The unexpected agenda item raised my curiosity about the rest of the workshop, but it also made me feel somewhat insecure; however, surprises appeared to be a recurring component of the workshop.

During the coffee break, I surveyed the group to get a sense of what kind of people were attending. During this, and later seminars, I found out that everybody, from a person on Social Security to a millionaire, attends these workshops. One could already guess that by looking at the cars in the parking lot. Only you never figure out who is who. Everybody is wearing T-shirts and leggings or jogging pants and, during the seminar, you focus on and talk about more important things than such inconsequential topics as professions.

So we were simply fifty people with different personalities. That's all I could figure out during the coffee break.

Following were four days full of surprises. Besides the meditations, trance journeys, etc., there was an incredible diversity of activities, more or less complex, and involving one, two, or more people: games for adults, drawing, singing, dancing, laughing. One can't name the multitude of vehicles we tried.

One evening we were to stand as close together as humanly possible in the middle of the room, the tallest people in the center. We were then supposed to come up with one common humming sound. There we were, standing as close as herrings and humming. Then the whole group started to sway back and forth. It was impossible to just stand still because the whole group was swaying in unison. It was an incredible feeling of unity.

When we were done humming, we were supposed to lie or sit down in the exact spot where we had been standing. But we were already standing like sardines with everyone's feet touching. The result was a huge, intertwined and knotted pile of people: Feet poking up from under arms, legs going over and under other legs, limbs everywhere, a total tangle of limbs. Then, to finish this session and conclude the evening, Gudrun played a recording of "Brahms' Lullaby" sung by a tenor. And, as incredible as it may sound, in this relaxed mood, after a full and action-packed day, the entire assembly sang along: all those fifty completely different people with such vastly different personalities. In the atmosphere of the workshop we had simply grown so close that we were, in fact, just lying on the floor together and singing "Brahms' Lullaby."

One of the exercises right at the beginning of the workshop had involved walking up to someone for whom we had an initial dislike or discomfort, or with whom we had wanted to interact the least. And we were supposed to talk to this person. At first, of course, I didn't feel quite comfortable with this exercise at all. But when, after some time had passed, the person whom I had mentally ostracized the most was still sitting by himself, I gathered all my courage and walked up to him. After our conversation, I still had the impression that he wasn't a person to whom I could relate much. But I found the awkward way in which he had interacted with me very human and somewhat touching, so much so that my aversion to him had totally vanished.

Not too long after that we were all lying with our eyes closed, on our blankets, following a guided trance journey, and were supposed to blindly search for a hand next to us and hold it, while listening to the singing of a mantra. The hand that I caught to my left felt incredibly warm and comfortably familiar. When we finally all opened our eyes again, I realized to my great surprise whose hand I had held: for indeed, it belonged to the unlikable guy, my "aversion-man."

But this isn't the end of the story; not yet. The

story has a sequel. Toward the end of the work-shop, we all wrote a letter to ourselves describing how we were doing right now, what we had experienced, and what resolutions for the future we had made. This letter would then be mailed to us three months later.

One workshop participant felt like sharing his letter with the group. He said that he had arrived at this workshop feeling totally alienated from himself, in a state of mind where he didn't know himself any more. He, therefore, had written a very formal and distant letter to himself: "Dear Mr. X, do you actually know what an arrogant and presumptuous son of a bitch you are? There is nothing real about you, no substance. You are noth-ing but a facade, always making those funny gags, always having to be the center of attention . . ."

The letter went on like this for a while, until he started talking about his experiences during the workshop, and the letter finished with the words: ". . . and finally I have you back, my dear, dear John!" Well, who do you think fell into each other's arms, totally moved and crying? The "aversion-man" and I. The experience was really incredible, and I cannot convey to you how much it has meant to me.

I could now write an entire book about this workshop and what I have experienced and learned through it. But I think that whoever feels touched by this report and gets curious enough, or is simply in the mood for experiencing minor and major "miracles," will go ahead and find out, personally, about the possibilities.

Everyone who has attended the four days of the workshop gets transformed. Too many miracles take place not to be. You re-learn how to be a human being, and experience that, in the end, people are really not that different from each other, regardless of age, origin, or upbringing. But most of all, this kind of experience is a very powerful step toward rediscovering yourself and reconnecting with your inner being and better nature!

10

A Detailed Description of the Cosmic Ordering Process

When a person can make a wish without worry or attachment to the outcome, the wish will immediately be granted.

Some yoga enthusiasts try to go into a trance by hanging upside down from their feet in order to reach a state in which they can program their unconscious to manifest the things they want in their lives. But the truth is: if you *think* you need a complicated ritual to "call up" the universe, then, by definition, you do; otherwise, you don't!

However, if you "order" with the universe in a totally unsuspecting and matter-of-fact way, and then forget about the order all together, you will get the best results. You can, for example, write down your order and in the middle of the night

read it to the universe through your
or from your porch, if that better fits
tic inclination. If you feel funny about p
order with the universe and think that no
be able to hear you, imagine that you are
into an imaginary cell phone that has a direct
nection to the universe.

That's it. Done!

This is an essential point: It is important that
you are, indeed, completely done with the order.
Avoid going back the next day and secretly thinking to yourself: "Hey, you guys up there in the
heavens, did anyone even listen to me last night?
Just to be on the safe side, here is my order again."
Two hours later: "Maybe it will work even better if
I send along some extra energy for my order." Just
before going to sleep: "And don't forget, you guys
on high . . . are you sure you've gotten my order
right?" A week later: "Is my order on its way, yet?
Hello, Universe, can you hear me?" . . . or whatever you may be thinking. Just think about what
the underlying concept is when you do these
things. You are assuming that the universe can't do
its job and is bungling your order. Otherwise you
wouldn't constantly be calling up there and check-
ing on it.

You should scrap your doubts around these as-
of-yet unexplained energies, and instead treat the
universe no worse than any other ordering service.
Furthermore, the universe is not a guru to whom
you go to beg and whine (which, by the way, gurus
don't like, either), but an energy source. Imagine
for a minute that you have mailed an order to one

'r companies, and the fol-
m a fax to confirm that
"hen you follow up with
ne three more times. A
may tolerate this kind
э you in their files for
want your money.

...se work a little dif-
...anifests through your belief,
, uur lack of doubts, and through the
...ss of mentally letting go and forgetting your order. The act of forgetting the order and letting go of your attachment to the outcome of the order is the safest bet for "beginners," since, based on lack of experience, they haven't yet developed the level of trust that is necessary for a successful ordering practice. The act of forgetting the order has the advantage that you, consequently, don't even think about having doubts or worries about the outcome.

You have to discover the best way of letting go of your attachment to the outcome of your order for yourself. One possible letting go practice involves telling yourself: "I love the way things are right now, and I don't need what I ordered in order to be happy. It is not important whether I receive what I ordered or not. I, hereby, am not sending off any duplicate orders to the universe and am not being a pest to the Ones On High. I am content with the way things are now, anyhow." Repeat these thoughts to yourself whenever you catch yourself re-sending an order or placing high expectations on the outcome of the order.

Strong attachment to the outcome of an order,

and high expectations, block the flow of the energy. The cosmic ordering service does not deliver via UPS, you know, but rather through inspiration. The inspiration often consists of only a tiny impulse or an intangible gut feeling that directs you to do one thing or another, or something along these lines. If you, however, already have high expectations, or are tense, sad, or doubtful about the outcome of your order, or impatiently waiting for the delivery, you can't hear your inner voice any more. This is the only, but very real, problem. Take it easy with cosmic ordering. Have fun, and everything else will follow! And: Don't blame yourself for being "order-placementally challenged," if it doesn't work out right away.

I had a definite advantage over you all with respect to cosmic ordering. When I placed my first order, I didn't think at all about what I was doing and whether the order would actually arrive. The only reason I ordered with the universe was to end the argument I was having with my friend at the time, so I didn't invest any emotional energy into doubts, worries, or high expectations at all. In fact, I had no expectations whatsoever, only a wonderful surprise when the order was delivered. With this feeling of success behind me, it was naturally much easier to continue on with the ordering service.

That's the trick, really. *One* spectacular success and things are rolling, because you believe in it then. Maybe you can try the following to facilitate the initial ordering process: If you have a car, you can practice by ordering a parking space. If you have to go somewhere where available parking space is usually scarce, order one for yourself before you leave home.

Maybe it so happens that somebody calls and you get delayed a little, that you are in the mood for taking a different route to your destination, or that you miss a green traffic light because you were distracted for a moment. In any case, you arrive at your destination and at the very moment you show up, somebody is leaving and freeing up a parking space thirty yards away from the place where you need to be going.

And up to this day you *always* had to go around the block at least three times to find a space, and ended up parking a great distance away. Acknowledge, at least, that this could have been a successful first order!

Acknowledgement is important. Suppose, for example, the employees in the Sears shipping department mailed you the beautiful sweater you had ordered from them, and you call them up eventually to say: "Well, to be honest, I am not so sure any more whether I haven't already owned this sweater for years, and am wondering if your delivery is actually still outstanding. I kind of think that I really haven't received a sweater from you, yet." The Sears employees would find your behavior rather ungrateful and would most likely not make you one of their favorite clients. If you, however, accidentally thank the universe twice for a delivery, even though the alleged order was actually only a coincidence (if there is such a thing), then the Ones On High will probably be so moved by your gratefulness that they will deliver the perfect parking space to you the next time you need one, even if you didn't explicitly order one. Furthermore, you are doing yourself a favor if you acknowledge (at least the possibility) that you were able to place a successful order. You will then be less afraid of failure when you order the next time.

While you are waiting for the delivery, consciously make the *decision* that the fulfillment of the order is not important and that you can love your life even without the thing you ordered. This kind of attitude actually speeds up the delivery; but I didn't really tell you this, because you are not supposed to be waiting for the delivery, right?

Disease—A Special Chapter in Ordering Etiquette

If you want to place an order to discontinue or cancel a disease, you have to phrase your order in a positive way (as is true for every other order, too). You don't "cancel" your headache, but rather order a clear, healthy, pain-free head, or something along these lines. The delivery often takes place either through a casual remark somebody makes that puts you in touch with a special healing modality that is right for you, or the delivery happens through a poignant experience that, at first sight, may not be entirely comfortable. Maybe through this incident you get pointed to the mental-emotional root of your disease, to what is really the cause of your headaches, and why your thoughts and emotions manifest themselves as headaches. In James Redfield's *The Celestine Prophecy*, this is described very well in the tenth prophecy; but I highly recommend that you read the entire book, starting with the first prophecy, otherwise you won't be able to make any sense of this concept!

Once you understand the cause of your disease and remember what you really want in life, and you start taking care of your "inner self" by creating a life that allows you to express yourself to the fullest degree, then your body won't have to continually remind you of the fact that you are neglecting yourself, and the disease will disappear. Lotions and salves are just crutches and attack only the symptoms of a disease. There are, however, treatments—for example, Bach Flower Remedies—that address the psychic reasons behind the disease and focus on drawing your attention to them. Maybe you will be guided toward those kinds of treatments by the ordering service.

In any case, I have now hereby officially warned you: "Canceling" diseases can raise the stress level in your life. The result of your proper, positive order could be a realization of the causes of your disease. But don't forget that you can always order more help to deal with this new awareness. So, it can't be all that bad, right? I only mention it because I have never experienced a case where someone's disease simply disappeared and did not involve some hard work on the sick person's part. People received only the necessary information regarding what needs to be done.

Summary

1. Order however and wherever works best for you. If you prefer to perform some sort of a small ritual, think of one that *you* believe in or that appears to be powerful for you. For example: Write down your order and read it to the universe at night from your open window, porch, garden, etc. Maybe you do this at a time when you are in an especially cheerful mood and have strong faith in your ordering abilities, or when you are simply feeling good about yourself and your life. If you like the full moon, order when the moon is full.

2. Place each order only once. (Keep in mind that you also have the possibility of canceling your order, if you wish). If you place the same order multiple times, or, in your mind, send extra energy numerous times to be on the safe side, you presuppose that the universe is incapable of handling your order correctly the first time. It doesn't really matter to the universe, but the Ones On High might find your behavior rather pitiful because . . .

3. . . . you receive the delivery as inspiration, through a gut feeling, through something somebody says accidentally or in passing, or through similarly intangible mechanisms. In this way, you can, at the appropriate time, be guided in a variety of ways to the right place where you can then receive your order. If you are too attached to the outcome or have high expectations, you are standing in your own way and block the free flow

of energy, so that the universe is constantly trying to catch you to deliver your order, but you never show up at the place of the delivery because you are too stressed out about the timely delivery.

4. Phrase every order in a positive way! Words like "not" and "no" are disadvantageous. For example, you wouldn't call up Sears to tell them: "I don't want to order a green tablecloth." Order that which you would like to have or have happen instead. If you would like to "cancel" a disease, you have to order health for the respective body part.

5. Acknowledge when an order is filled successfully. In this way, you raise your level of faith in your ordering capabilities. If you are not sure whether the granting of your wish was just a coincidence or not, at least acknowledge that the outcome might possibly have been a successful cosmic ordering attempt. Especially clever ordering enthusiasts place orders with the following reservation in mind: "It could be possible that the order will get delivered completely coincidentally right at the time I am requesting. What a coincidence, indeed!" It doesn't matter how it works; what's important is that it does work! As mentioned before: Take it easy, have fun and everything else will follow.

6. If you would like to bring an overall positive flow into your life, make a list of how things would be and how you would feel if everything in your life were exactly as you wanted it. Then determine which areas of your life currently

deviate from the things on the list. Write reminders of things on this list on little note cards and stick them all over your house and office; and, whenever you come across one of the notes, think about whether what you are presently saying, thinking, and feeling is bringing you any closer to the image of the optimal person you want to be and the life you are seeking. Remember: Your words, thoughts, and feelings create your reality!

When you have caught yourself, a few times, talking, thinking, or feeling negatively and unproductively: First, stop being surprised about the content of your present reality, and second, at the very moment you realize this, you start the process of awakening to a new reality. You begin to consciously create your life and place your orders. You have reached the end of your long hibernation! The only difference between an awake and a sleeping person is that the first creates his reality consciously and the latter does so unconsciously.

"Know yourself," said the Oracle of Delphi. Take this a little further and it becomes: "Decide who and how you want to be!" Because, once you realize what creates your reality, you need no longer be attached to it. You can choose something new for yourself. You can, therefore, also decide what kind of a person you want to be and how you want to live.

11

What Is Happening in the Afterworld? Does It Even Exist?

Some near-death experiences—provided that you can accept that they aren't outright, hair-raising fairy tales—present convincing evidence that "the other side" is just as lively a place as this reality. The following is a summary of some excerpts from a book by Elisabeth Kübler-Ross, one of the leading researchers of near-death experiences. These excerpts may provide additional insights into the workings of the "cosmic shipping department team." The reader may form his or her own opinion.

Kübler-Ross explains: "By nature, I am a skeptical semi-believer [in God], to put it mildly. As such, I was not interested in exploring questions around the possibility of a life after death. But certain events that kept repeating themselves didn't leave me any choice but to pay attention to this possibility."

Kübler-Ross was drawn to the topic of life after death through experiences with patients who, after having been declared dead for as long as forty-five minutes, started to show signs of life again. These patients had not only clearly heard every word that had been spoken while they were "dead," but could also read and later repeat the thoughts of everybody in the room. During the following years of directed research in this field, Kübler-Ross looked specifically for cases that would provide convincing, sound, and solid evidence for the existence of life after death.

The Blind Regain Their Vision

Kübler-Ross interviewed a number of completely blind people with respect to their near-death experiences. As with everyone else, the blind, too, saw themselves in an out-of-body state floating over their physical body and calmly observing their death. The interesting thing is that all the blind people could in this state see again, and could give detailed descriptions of the clothes people in the room were wearing, including the patterns of ties, colors of sweaters, etc.

Another interesting aspect is that the dying, while leaving their bodies, were aware of the presence of non-physical, etheric beings surrounding them, and often perceived the presence of already deceased relatives.

That means that nobody, absolutely nobody, dies alone; and that includes a "lonely" astronaut in space, who is as physically isolated as one can get. (Please, read this paragraph to Granny, too, so she won't worry about dying alone! But only if she wants to hear about these things, although most grannies and granddads are interested in this stuff.)

In order to find more convincing, sound evidence, Kübler-Ross went to a children's hospital, specifically on those days when the weather was especially good, and families were expected to be on the road to enjoy an outing; and so were more likely to be involved in fatal accidents. She then sat by the side of the children who had been rushed into the emergency room. Shortly before dying, a state of peaceful solemnity spread over each child, which generally points to a profound emotional experience.

At this moment, Kübler-Ross asked the children if they were willing and able to tell her about their current experiences. And they would, for example, reply: "Everything is okay. Mommy and Peter are already waiting for me!" In this case, the mother had passed away at the scene of the accident, as Kübler-Ross already knew, but little Peter was supposedly still alive and being treated at another children's hospital. A moment later, the other hospital called with the information that little Peter had passed on fifteen minutes earlier. The child had known this before Kübler-Ross.

In another example, a Native American woman, run over by a car, was "picked up" by her father who lived 600 miles away. As Kübler-Ross found out later, the father had died of a heart attack only an hour before, which the woman could not have known before her accident.

Kübler-Ross talks about these and many other examples in her book, *On Death and Dying*.

12

"E.T. Phone Home . . ."

The following exercise is very popular in eso-teric circles. I am printing it here because some people, after being confronted with the thoughts of Kübler-Ross, or after being successful at, for example, bending spoons with their minds, are now searching for a contact to "the other side behind the veil." The evidence points more and more to the fact that there is something there. Now we want to touch the untouchable!

For some people, the following exercise has produced amazing results, greatly exceeding the expectations one has when reading the simple instructions. It doesn't hurt to try it out; maybe you are one of the people who will succeed in "contacting the other side."

Purely logical and rational people should either turn off their minds for this exercise and get ready for a children's imagination game, or not even attempt to follow this exercise at all. However, the "ordering mechanism" works even if all this exercise does for you is make your hair stand up on end. So don't let your resistance stop you. You have the right to be happy and the right to create your happiness in whatever way you please.

Close your eyes and imagine you are standing in a place in nature that symbolizes peace and broad expanse for you. It could be a mountaintop overlooking the surrounding land for a long distance; a beach from which you can see the ocean would do, too. Imagine the peace and quiet there until a feeling of safety and security, a feeling of wellness, peace, and lightness, settles in. Maybe it would help if, in your mind, you went back in time to an event in which you felt especially calm, peaceful, and sheltered, to evoke these feelings for this exercise.

When these feelings have settled in and you are really comfortable and relaxed, start imagining, in the distance, the misty veil that exists between you and the spiritual world. It could also look like a dark curtain, depending on which image works best for you.

Then you see the veil, no matter whether it looks misty or dark, coming slowly toward you, and you are already looking forward to reaching it. Imagine that the home of your soul is drawing near.

Should you have problems with this image or with producing this mental picture, pull out your ordering list and request help to facilitate the imagination process, or ask for a clue about which image would work best for you. Whatever you request, it will be delivered.

When the veil has drawn very close to you, let it stop. Reach through it with your hands, either quickly or slowly, depending on your own preference, to greet your spiritual guide on the other side. You can either reach out physically or only in your imagination. Keep your hands extended and reaching for a while, and wait.

After a few moments, different things happen for different people. Some people are so overwhelmed with emotions that they start crying. It is as if for your entire life you thought you were alone, but suddenly it feels as though you are surrounded by beings who are much closer and dearer to you than anything or anybody you have ever known before. You then realize that in every second of your life, your dearest friends have stood right next to you. You had only to reach out and communicate with them.

For others, only the fingers tingle or their hands warm up during the first time. Or something completely different happens. Let yourself be open for a surprise. The more child-like your attitude is toward this game, the more successful this exercise will be for you. You can do this exercise daily, but do it for only a few minutes; for the harder you want to hang on to this wonderful new feeling, the faster it will vanish.

13

Tips for Everyday Life

Following is a list of tips, bits of advice, and wise sayings or excerpts, including fragments of spiritual knowledge, spiritual laws, and laws of fate. They present a checkered mixture and are meant as reminders to help you create a full and active life. You could, for example, keep this guide to the Cosmic Ordering Service next to your bed and every time you are in the mood for another piece of advice, open it up to this chapter of the book, read some of the tips and go to sleep with them; or get up with them in the morning. Whichever you prefer.

If we want to consciously create our life and

not miss the delivery of our orders through sleeping or other distractions, then it is necessary for us to stay conscious. That's what this varied mixture of suggestions is supposed to do: Keep alive the knowledge and awareness of your own truth, and the ever-present, all-encompassing confidence that a wonderful being who loves life is either slumbering inside of you or is all awake. It doesn't matter if you cannot yet see this clearly and accept it.

As a reminder: Researchers have found that it is impossible to have negative thoughts when you are relaxed; and no baby is born into this world stressed, trying to be cool, or with low self-esteem. Your natural state is joy, love, and abundance in everything. Everything else is artificial and an error.

Here they are, the tips for everyday life. Some of them may "talk" to you more than others. Enjoy the ones that work for you!

* *There is no way to happiness, happiness is the way.*
—Buddha

* *Our true business is to be happy.*
—Dalai Lama

* *Death is an optical illusion.*
—Albert Einstein

* *It is better to light the smallest light than to moan about the general darkness.*
—Confucius

* *Truth has to be repeated time and again, as also the errors of the world are preached time and again, in fact, not by one or two, but by the masses.*
—Johann Wolfgang von Goethe

✳ A problem means FOR YOU, as, were it
    against you, it would be called a contra-blem.
                                        —Dieter Hörner

✳ Fears and anxieties make sense only if you
    believe that something outside of yourself is cre-
    ating your reality. Without this conviction fear
    does not make any sense.
                                        —Bodo Deletz

(The rest of the quotes are mine.)

✳ Those who always assume the worst from life
    are critical in a stupid way. Those who always
    assume the best from life are naive in an intelli-
    gent way.

✳ Many problems are in fact only missed moments
    of happiness.

✳ What makes you happier: To deal with what you
    want and to increase it, or to deal with what you
    do not want and to fight against it?

✳ It's your choice and your free will to decide
    whether a rainy day is a good day or a bad day.
    Rain in itself is actually as beautiful as anything else.
    It is fresh, it cleans the air, it gives a lush hue to
    nature, and it is ideal for a comfortable bath in the
    bathtub.

✳ When you increase the quality of your life, life
    will increase the quantity of the quality!

✳ Follow your sense of well-being. When you do not
    feel well with an idea, then you have not yet dis-
    covered the truth.

❋   From the small moments of happiness you can train not to miss the big ones!

❋   It is good to practice being happy daily, otherwise you might faint from fright with "too much luck at once," and only wake up when the opportunity has passed.

❋   Better to rejoice once too often (about a universal delivery that proved to be coincidence, for example) than one time too few.

❋   A problem without a solution cannot exist, just as a medal with but one side cannot exist, because then it would be a medal no more.

❋   When you focus too much on problems you become blind to the beautiful moments of life.

❋   The Divine Will is always that which wants me to make my life a paradise on Earth. When I, by virtue of my own free will, decide to be a wet blanket, then I have to play this role alone without help from "above."

❋   Those who have too much fear of bad things, miss the good ones. Those who have too much fear of death, miss life.

❋   Those who, daily, grab at the little chances and opportunities, also seize the spontaneous big chances unflappably and unhesitatingly. But those who have never trained and were only waiting for the one big chance will become nervous and stand under pressure to perform, and won't know what to do when the big chance occurs. Too soon it is gone.

✳ A big chance in life is like crossing a small ocean. After you have done it, it might well be that your horizon will have changed completely and many things are different. Therefore, you should have learned before how to swim, to ride a boat, or to sail.

✳ Even when you have crossed many oceans you will find out that thereby you do not become a different person, you only receive different opportunities. But to seize them on either side of the ocean is still up to you.

✳ Life magnifies everything you do: When you enjoy the small good things in life, life will ensure that you also thrive on a larger scale. But when you moan, grumble, sleep through, and ignore the little wonders of life, life will provide that on a large scale, as well, and you will have enough reason to moan and grumble.

If you do a good job (on a small scale), then life also will do its job well (on a large scale), as life sees your "guidelines" as an expression of what you want and follows your will "obediently!"

✳ The difference between a "big" and a "small" miracle exists only in your mind, as does the difference between a small and a big cosmic order.

When someone living in the desert sees snow for the first time, it is a big miracle for him. He hears the snow, he feels it, he tastes it, and he perceives it with all his senses.

When someone living in the mountains sees snow, he does not even perceive it, as for him, it is something quite ordinary.

Make it an exercise to perceive things with all your senses, as if you were seeing them for the first time.

When you are able to again experience all the little miracles as big ones, then the miracles are all equally big, and this makes the delivery of all your orders equally probable.

✳ It is totally unnecessary to solve problems and difficulties of all sorts alone. When you are in contact with your inner voice (not always, but increasingly often), the entirety of the universal wisdom will always stand by you with a helping hand.

When you are looking for new ideas do not ask your mind, ask your heart and your sense of well-being.

When difficult conversations lie ahead, do not discuss with your intellect, but with your heart, and believe that there is always a solution that makes everybody content.

✳ You can be lazy in an intelligent or in a stupid way.

The stupid lazybones cause themselves more trouble, while the intelligent lazybones increase their efficiency, and so have less work.

It is also silly to do everything alone and to be too lazy to cultivate your contact with the inner voice. This only causes more trouble.

It is intelligent to always be nice to your inner voice, because then you can be creative together with the universe. This is true efficiency.

(Of course, you may also be diligent, but, unfortunately, I do not know much about that.)

✳ Love for the entirety of creation is the key to becoming yourself a fully aware creator, as love provides that we stop creating undesirable things unconsciously.

✳   Each person has the individual prerequisites for a happy and satisfying life, provided that he knows himself as completely as possible. How happy would a sheep be, going to a school for wolves and trying to become a good wolf, or vice versa?

Thoughts and feelings are like little viruses: They multiply with enormous speed. Still, you may decide whether it will become a good-mood virus or a grumble-grouse one.

✳   Each thought is a trigger. You decide whether you want to trigger good things or bad.

✳   The most intelligent thing you can do is to appreciate everything, no matter how bad it is. It won't take long before life will give up. It will adapt to your mind and will only deliver good things. This is so because you design your reality with your free will. You design reality by what you think about it, and you have the free will to think whatever you want.

This is no far-out, esoteric philosophy, but also modern quantum physics. Man creates reality through expectation. Expect things to be bad, and they will be bad and will become even worse. Expect things to be good, and they will be good and will become even better. If you don't believe me, then test this on your fellow human beings. On Mondays expect the worst of everybody, on Tuesdays, the best. On which day are people nicer?

✳   Love the bad and the good has to come.

Love all "stupid" persons (always on second rank after yourself), and they will become nicer and nicer.

Love all difficult situations, and they will become easier and easier.

✳ What you secretly fear is the first thing to come. So be clever and always expect the best. When something does not work, always conclude from this that the next opportunity will be better.

✳ That which you can order innocently, as guile-lessly as a child, works like an express order with the universe. It will come immediately.

✳ Reality exists only in the eye of the beholder.

✳ How do I manage to love everything the way it is?
   Very simply: you care for the small things in life—What do I want to wear today? Whom do I want to meet? What do I want to think about the other person; how do I want to treat her? What do I want to see, hear, read, taste, feel? Where do I want to go? Which sort of tea do I want to drink? On which seat do I want to sit?—and life and the universe will care for the whole picture (optimal job, health, friends, partner; abundance in all areas of life).
   When you provide a blissful and comfortable life in respect to the minor areas of life, then life will regulate the big things accordingly, and with the same basic feeling; for example, nice and com-fortable, if this is your guideline within the small things.

✳ The difference between small and big orders exists only in our minds. Life doesn't care whether we order a spontaneous healing, as it happens in Lourdes quite often (as of today, 2,000 medically accepted, miraculous healings have happened there, and the number still increases), or a free parking lot in the city. The difference exists only within ourselves.

* For a first step toward "creatively designing one's own life with universal help," it is totally sufficient to be merely open for the possibility. The more you trust in this over time, the faster your wishes will come true.

* It is a good trick to start every morning with thoughts of gratefulness. Even if, on the first day, you cannot think of more than: "I am grateful that the sun has risen again and that there is still enough air to breathe," you will notice that the list of things for which you can be grateful will, wondrously, become longer and longer every morning.

* Those who have made the universe their business partner and their best friend and coach, save a lot of time, trouble, expense, and effort. You can deal with more things in less time and gain more free time, more sense of achievement, and a better mood.

* Too much brooding and too much knowledge hinder the decision-making process. This is also what an article from a German women's magazine says about some research by the Max Planck Institute for Education Research in Berlin. According to the report, among the 1,600 persons tested, those who had only trusted in their intuition had, in general, all achieved better results, even in their choice of stocks. So be clever and trust your intuition. When you further tell your mind that via its logic-orientated brain-half it can only perceive seven impressions per second, while intuition via its image-oriented brain-half can pick up 10,000 impressions in the same time, then even the most critical mind will find it logical and reasonable to "shut-up" more often and let intuition go first.

✳ Intuition just has access to a far bigger database than the mind has.

✳ The cosmic ordering service loves enthusiastic customers and sends many extra "free gifts" (nice, additional surprise deliveries) after them as an award, because nature is interested in happy people as they care more for nature and do not destroy her. This is like a "miles and more" discount. Depending on what "conditions" you have arranged for with the cosmic ordering service, there will be an extra delivery with every tenth order! (The "conditions" are only subject to your free will and that which you choose to believe in.)

✳ Clear intentions will bring clear (delivery) results.
When you are still thinking about your "big intentions" you can use the time to clearly formulate the "small ones." For example: Every day I want to have at least one nice conversation, be glad one time, to have laughed one time, etc.
Practice makes perfect, and some time in the future, your "big intentions" will become clearer.

✳ No baby is born at his wits' end, cool, or having an inferiority complex. Your natural state is joy, love, and abundance in every respect. Everything else is artificial and an error.

✳ Do you know who you are? Remember: Being at the end of one's tether, being cool and distant, having an inferiority complex: This cannot really be you.
So who are you at the core of your being? Every human being's soul is beautiful, but to show this beauty outwardly you must first have found it within you.

✳ What if it were all only a coincidence?

Counter question: What would this change?
When faith in the cosmic ordering service causes
someone to derive so much will to live that he or
she is in such a good mood that more and more
positive things result, totally by themselves . . .
isn't that wonderful? What, then, if the cosmic
ordering service really exists?

You take a big risk if you never try it out, as you
could possibly have saved much time and effort in
many areas of your life, for quite a long while, had
you only communicated more often, and sooner,
with your inner voice and the universe.
Even totally unenlightened people can do cosmic
ordering. (For evidence, see the author herself!)
We do not have to have reached enlightenment to
improve our lives, we need only to really and sin-
cerely get on our way with body, mind, and spirit,
and then life will come to meet us.

✳ Do you realize that researchers know that scientists
at universities influence the results of their experiments through their preconceptions and expectations? For this reason most experiments are
computer controlled, as the computer does not
have any expectations.

These scientists have neither worked with
autosuggestion nor do they meditate at length to
"learn" how to manipulate results. On the contrary: They do not do anything, and yet cannot
prevent it from happening.

Accordingly, it is not an acquired capacity to
influence reality with one's own expectations, but
an innate human characteristic. And this applies
also to you. When you expect not to have any
influence on your reality, then reality is so nice as
to present itself so that it looks as though you do,
in fact, have no influence upon it.

✴   When somebody is rejoicing and is deeply
     touched by something, we should participate in
     this joy—although that is often dismissed as sen-
     timental—as intensely as possible. When we
     begin to feel this joy at the view of any daisy, then
     we will notice with astonishment how things that
     we wish for just fall at our feet more and more
     often, and faster and faster.

✴   Thoughts of joy and love toward things result in
     faster deliveries of all my wishes and conscious
     orders, while doubtful thoughts or anger (no mat-
     ter about what or about whom) provide that
     even more reasons for doubt and anger will occur
     in my life. Every thought and every feeling multi-
     plies itself.

✴   What do you, in fact, expect? Do you know the
     prevailing result of the roughly 50,000 thoughts
     that you think per day? What are your prevailing
     expectations? Nobody is thinking only positively
     or only negatively. But what are you thinking? Do
     you think, for two-thirds of the day, that you do
     not have any effect on reality anyway; or do you
     think, for two-thirds of the day that, in the end,
     most things will happen the way you want them
     to? Or is your perception at least two-thirds neu-
     tral, and you think that this is, after all, possible
     and you are open for anything?
         When you are not sure about this, keep a
     thought-diary and write down every hour for
     two weeks what you have just been thinking. Be
     honest with yourself and make a note of every-
     thing. After these two weeks, you will know what
     your true expectations are.

✳   You do not believe that your thoughts have the ability to create your own reality? But you would like to believe it, as you see that it is a reasonable assumption? Then please be kind to yourself and feed your mind daily with information—from books, conversations, lectures—that shows that man can indeed have some effect through his expectations, and that it is stupid to expect other than the best from life! Make a list of all your positive experiences, and of all those tiny coincidences that give you further reason for the assumption that you do have an effect on your reality.

✳   If your cosmic ordering does not yet work properly, although it is inevitable that everyone really has an effect on their reality through their expectations, then this only proves one thing: that you are not yet nice enough toward yourself! When you feel better about and better understand yourself, and know your deepest needs and your deepest sources of joy, then you will also feel and perceive your inner voice more clearly, and it will guide you increasingly often to the right place at the right time to receive the deliveries of your cosmic orders from the universe!

✳   Everything that you reject and condemn will get in the way of your "express deliveries." On the other hand, love toward all things makes them come true much faster. Maybe it is helpful for you to know that you do not have to reject and condemn everything that you do not want in order to live. To the contrary: The less you condemn these things, or persons, the less you will have to face them when they do not suit you.

✳   If I want to go to Rome, I first have to know where I am right now to know how I might get there. Do I need a boat next because I am standing at a river's edge, or do I need a cable railway next because I am standing at the foot of a mountain?

When I want to become rich, happy, etc., it is equally useful to know where I am, how I am, and what could be my next step. As soon as I am on my way in the right direction, the "street signs" will come toward me on their own.

✳   It is not tragic when you order and receive things that you yet cannot use. To the contrary: This accelerates self-knowledge and self-development enormously because in that way you do not continue to think for years, "Oh, had I finally this and that." That is, the things you have already ordered and received and then realized were, as yet, totally unnecessary.

Apart from that, even the most unnecessary order is still good and necessary for something: That is, to strengthen your faith that the cosmic ordering service still exists.

✳   At the beginning of our journeys toward gaining self-knowledge, we often assume that a horrible monster lives in the depth of our souls. But as soon as we begin to discover the truth in the minor things of our everyday lives (for example: Do I prefer to drink green or black tea today?), we find out that the dreadful monster has only been a terribly scared pussycat that nobody has caressed for quite a long time.

✳   Each person's soul is whole, like that of a newborn baby. Equally, the sky behind the clouds is always blue (the clouds stand for everything from little problems to big neuroses). If you think negatively of yourself and your abilities, then you see yourself too superfluously. Because of all the clouds, you do not see the blue sky of your soul anymore. Be ensured that it is there, nonetheless.

✳ When somebody does something stupid it is only because he cannot think of something better in that moment. You should not take the shortcomings of others too personally, but take care of your own abilities instead.

✳ There is no reason to make more effort than you enjoy.

✳ Straining retards the self-discovery process. Having fun accelerates it! There are many therapeutic approaches that see this differently, but you should decide for yourself.

✳ When somebody has realized that mental forces and invisible powers exist, this is no proof of this person being a good person. It only proves that anyone can reach this understanding without being enlightened.

✳ Do you think it would be sensible to assume and believe the opposite of that which you want to have? Is it not much wiser to always expect the best?

✳ Only rarely is a situation in itself the problem. Mostly the real problem is how we think about the situation.

✳ One person can be totally happy about the same external circumstances that make another person totally unhappy. Only by making this clear to yourself will many problems disappear into thin air, and uncounted moments of happiness will not pass you by.

✳ When you see that the full responsibility for your problems lies within yourself, it is quite easy to solve them.

✳ Problems are not there to be discussed, but to be solved.

✳ When you are in a hurry, you are not open for creative impulses. Therefore, hurry and frantic pace never really save time.

✳ Someone who moves through life totally relaxed, from his own inner core, will have enough time for all intuitive impulses.

✳ It is wise to learn to discern an inner sense of well-being, which is derived from your soul from that which comes from superfluous contentment.

I might, for example, be superfluously content because I have taken revenge for something; or I might feel truly good, from the bottom of my heart, because I have found a solution from which everybody profits and which also strengthens my self-esteem.

✳ Somebody who knows that his true aim in life is only to be happy is able to give preference to wisdom and does not need to insist on ignorance.

✳   Bad mood on a rainy day?

     Maybe your inner voice prescribes you pepper-mint tea with raspberry ice cream against inner chaos. So what? This is great advice! I would accept it immediately as, this way, nothing can go wrong.

✳   You may go on a holiday trip halfway around the world, but if you do not really feel well at heart, nowhere else will you recover.

✳   Considering all the suffering on Earth, many people ask themselves time and again what this God in heaven actually is doing, except for having siesta. Others believe that he has given each of us the power to avoid all of this suffering. But we often use our free will to not use this power.

✳   The main difference between an unconscious and a conscious person is that the unconscious one mostly reacts automatically, while the conscious one has the freedom to react consciously, according to his decision in any given moment. This is a difference like that between a remote-controlled toy and the person operating the remote control. The person in control has the impression that he, himself, has all the power in life, while the other will think that he is subject to given circumstances and to fate. The only reason for the latter lies within the automatic reactions that result from too little awareness of the present.

✳   Energy follows attention. Notice the beauty and it will multiply. Notice all the situations where you managed to finish something especially good and easy and they will multiply. Notice and acknowledge when something comes easily to you: When you want butter, and somebody puts it in front of you; when the phone rings, and you know who it is before you have even picked up. When you acknowledge and appreciate such things happening, they will happen more often in all areas of life.

✳ Everything that a person sends out in words or through deeds will come back to him. He will receive what he has given.

✳ If you wish for something without worrying about it, it will come immediately.

(The following quotes are by the German writer and coach Bodo Deletz.)

✳ Imagine you would feel really great with a thing that is actually "bad." How would you know that it is actually something bad?

✳ Rejection suppresses all creativity. If you really want to do something good for the world, then focus your perception on the beauty. This will increase your creativity and also your desire to experience the beauty more often. It will be much easier for you to get rid of problems and you will have fun doing it.

✳ You are never really happy because you have solved a problem, but because you have focused your perception on the feeling of being happy. This you can do always.

✳ People believe they must direct their perception

onto the ugly in order to get rid of it, while they actually want to experience only the beautiful. That way they almost never come to experience the good feelings, as they are, instead, too busy fighting back with their negative feelings. People experience positive feelings only when they do not find any further reason to perceive the negative. If people were not so diligently seeking the source of their unhappiness and fighting against it, they would automatically be happy.

✳ Love does not need to be evoked. It just is and can be perceived. But this only works when your perception is, in fact, focused on this feeling. Through your fears you focus your perception automatically on everything that might go wrong. You will always have the feelings that you direct your perception toward.

✳ Deep within us, we feel the urge for love and joy of living, but we are always firmly convinced that we can get this joy of living only from outside. This conviction creates all of our problems in life. Would we recognize that real love and joy of living are only to be found inside, we would have no problems.

(The following quotes are taken from Neale Donald Walsh's *Conversations with God*, Books 1, 2, and 3, also published by Hampton Roads Publishing Co., Inc.)

✳ Everything that is, can be used to construct who you really are.
Absent everything else, you are not.
—Conversations with God, Book 1

*   The most loving person is the person who is self-centered.
    If you cannot love yourself you cannot love another.
    —Conversations with God, Book 1

*   You can create who you are over and over again. Indeed, you do—every day. As things now stand, you do not always come up with the same answer [or the same ordering from the universe], however. Given an identical outer experience, on day one you may choose to be patient, loving, and kind in relationship to it. On day two you may choose to be angry, ugly, and sad.
    The Master is one who always comes up with the same answer—and that answer is always the highest choice.
    —Conversations with God, Book 1

*   In case of any problems of any kind only one question is relevant, only one question is meaningful, only one question has any importance to your soul: What would love do now? [Love of self in the first place!]
    —Conversations with God, Book 1

*   The soul speaks to you in feelings.
    —Conversations with God, Book 2

*   Decide who you are—who you want to be—and then do everything in your power to be that!
    —Conversations with God, Book 2

*   Why does it take so much time to create the reality you choose? This is why: because you have not been living your truth.
    —Conversations with God, Book 2

✳ When you express your truth with love, negative and damaging results rarely occur.
—Conversations with God, Book 2

✳ Negativity is never a sign of ultimate truth. It only arises out of an unhealed part of you.
—Conversations with God, Book 2

✳ When you see things correctly, you become creative, rather than reactive.
When you come to each moment cleanly, without a previous thought about it, you can create who you are, rather than re-enact who you once were. Life is a process of creation, and you keep living it as if it were a process of re-enactment!
—Conversations with God, Book 2

✳ Previous experience is no indicator of truth, since pure truth is created here and now, not re-enacted.
The past and the future can exist only in thought. The pre-sent moment is the only reality. Stay there! There is only one moment—this moment—the eternal moment of now.
—Conversations with God, Book 2

✳ There is no evil! You are perfect, just as you are.
—Conversations with God, Book 2

✳ All of life is a process of deciding who you are, and then experiencing that.
—Conversations with God, Book 2

✳ You want the world to change? Change things in your own world.
—Conversations with God, Book 2

＊ *What you do not know is not so. Since you do not remember the future, it has not happened to you yet! A thing happens only when it is experienced. A thing is experienced only when it is known.*
—Conversations with God, Book 2

＊ *If you don't like what you sense about your future, step away from that! Just step away from it! In that instant you change your experience— and every one of you breathes a sigh of relief!*
—Conversations with God, Book 2

＊ You are in an eternal moment of self creation and self fulfillment through the process of self expression. Everyone is creating everything now being experienced—which is another way of saying that I am creating everything now being experienced, for I am everyone. THERE IS ONLY ONE OF US.
—Conversations with God, Book 2

＊ When you find inner peace, neither the presence nor the absence of any person, place or thing, condition, circumstance, or situation can be the creator of your state of mind or the cause of your experience of being.
—Conversations with God, Book 2

＊ Fear and guilt are your only enemies. Love and awareness are your true friends.
—Conversations with God, Book 3

＊ Happiness is a state of mind. And like all states of mind, it reproduces itself in physical form.
—Conversations with God, Book 3

Manifestation trick:

✳ If you choose to be happy, cause another to be happy.

If you choose to be prosperous, cause another to prosper.

If you choose more love in your life, cause another to have more love in theirs . . . .

The very act of your giving something away causes you to experience that you HAVE it to give away. Your mind comes to a new conclusion, a new thought, about you—namely, that you must have this, or you could not be giving it away.

So when you want something, give it away. You will then no longer be "wanting" it. You will immediately experience "having" it.

—Conversations with God, Book 3

✳ When your choices conflict—when body, mind, and spirit are not acting as one—the process of creation works at all levels, producing mixed results. If, on the other hand, your being is in harmony, and your choices are unified, astonishing things can occur.

—Conversations with God, Book 3

✳ Stop thinking of yourself as separate, and all the true power that comes from the inner strength of unity is yours!

Act as if you were separate from nothing, and no one, and you will heal your world tomorrow. This is the greatest secret of all time.

—Conversations with God, Book 3

✳ *The way to control your thoughts is to change
your perspective.*
　　　　　　　　　　　—*Conversations with God*, Book 3

This list could go on and on. I recommend that
you indulge in a few of the books in the following
list and mark with colored pencils those wise
words of advice that you enjoy the most, so you
can read them over and over again. Read one piece
of advice every day before you go to sleep and your
vibrations will remain at a high frequency and clar-
ity. The higher the frequency of your vibrations,
the better you can manifest what you want in life,
and the more successful your cosmic ordering
practice will become. Good luck and much success!

Recommended Reading

Walsch, Neale Donald. *Conversations with God, Books 1, 2, and 3.*

The author is trapped in crises in all conceivable aspects of life and writes a letter of complaint to God. Suddenly, his hand continues to write on its own and answers all the questions, unconventionally and ingeniously simple. All limiting concepts are resolved.

I have read each of the three books right up to the last page, and then immediately started once more at the beginning.

Kensington, Ella. Die 7 Botschaften unserer Seele (*The 7 Messages of Our Soul*; available in German only)

The chapter-headlines are:

1. I am what I experience.
2. I experience what I think.
3. I think what I feel.
4. I feel what I believe.
5. I believe what I want.

6. I want what I love.
7. I love what I am.

Similar to *Conversations with God*, human existence is explained in a practical and playful way, this time within the story of Bodo and Gina. Bodo gets in contact with his soul, which he consults on the events of the day each night, and his soul teaches him what he has to do in order to let each day of his life become a day of pure joy.

————. Mary
(*Mary*; available in German only)

The best book in the world against lovesickness and bad mood is called *Mary*, also by Ella Kensington. This time the knowledge is wrapped in an enchanting story: Michael, hopelessly in love and eaten up by self-doubts, has enough of only one thing in life: problems. His story and how he easily finds a positive attitude toward life (the optimal outlook for perfect cosmic orderers!) is linked with the story of a being from another world who comes to Earth in order to learn how to have problems. She has no clue how they should work, but they sound thrilling to her.

So, here they are: Michael, who has nothing but problems; and Mary, who cannot understand at all how she could finally learn to have a problem.

It is almost impossible to read this book and still have problems afterward. Günter, a friend of mine, called me three times during his reading to tell me where he just was and how great the book was. Not much later another friend of mine gave me a lecture that he had "only now" and "only through Günter" learned of this book, and why had I not told him about it earlier? In the meantime, Günter and Siegfried both drive around with at least fifteen copies of this book in their trunk so that they can recommend and give the book to anybody they meet. An absolute *Mary*-boom has broken out here.

———. Mysterio
(*Mysterio*; available in German only)

Hit number three by Ella Kensington is called *Mysterio*. After I had read *Mary*, I thought: "Well, she cannot write only great books; possibly this third one is not so good . . ." But obviously she can! I liked *Mysterio* as much as the others.

This time the story is about a computer game accidentally discovered on the Internet that first asks the player what she wishes for most in life. When the wish matches the rules of the game, the game grants it. That way the female protagonist suddenly receives three million dollars and her dream-man! Through the game, she learns that she herself creates her own reality with her thoughts, feelings, and words. This helps her to raise her consciousness so that her thoughts and feelings are realized faster and faster. But this is quite dangerous for, as soon she thinks something negative, it also comes true at once!

I found the book so thrilling that I was totally enchanted. It was as if I, myself, were already playing this magical game, "Mysterio," which makes happen that upon which we direct our perception: the game of life that we are actually always playing, even without noticing it.

Egli, Rene. *Das LOLA-Prinzip.*
(*The LOLA Principle;* available in German only)
LOLA is an acronym for letting go, love, and action/reaction. In a charming manner, the author makes the laws of life accessible to the reader.

Further, he makes clear why an increase of love in life does not affect man's performance and the attainment of his aims in a linear way, but in an exponential manner (analogous to Ohm's law); this comes, of course, with practical instructions and examples that illustrate what is said. Actually, this book is a *must*, too.

Shinn, Florence Scovel. *The Game of Life and How to Play It*.

The book is as nice as its title; a comprehensible summary of the rules of life, written in the first half of the 19th century. The author often uses quotes from the Bible, but ones that are not disturbing; it's rather surprising that there are still so many good things in the Bible version of today (at least I, as a non-denominational believer with only a dim recollection of my religious education in school, was positively surprised).

Mini-Course for 18 Days. Compiled from the work: *A Course in Miracles*.
(An instructional manual for healing relationships, and for reaching peace of mind.)

Golas, Thaddeus. *The Lazy Man's Guide to Enlightenment*.
(Out of print in English.)
"Learn to love hell and you are in heaven." Why and how, Thaddeus explains in a rather unconventional way. Recommended reading for all urban neurotics, freaks, creatives, and all those who enjoy an unusual perspective.

Kübler-Ross, Elisabeth. *On Death and Dying*.
(See chapter 11 of this book.)

Redfield, James. *The Celestine Prophecy.*

For those who do not yet know this book, it is high time! It's absolutely no coincidence that it became a bestseller. An adventure novel that reminds me of a saying:

> "Science is a structure built of facts,
> just as a house is a building of bricks.
> But as a pile of bricks is not a house,
> a pile of facts is not science."

The Celestine Prophecy is spiritual understanding wrapped in a wonderful building. A total work of art that helps one to understand and to remember many things that before were only grey theory. And it just reads sooooo well! An absolute *must* in your book list.

About the Author

Barbel Mohr was born in Bonn, Germany. She has worked as a photographer, editor, magazine designer, video producer, and author, gives "How to Have More Fun in Your Daily Life" workshops, and publishes her own German online-magazine.

Mohr travels widely in Germany to promote better living through her seminars and lectures. From 1998 to 2001, she published four German self-help books—including the best-selling *Bestellungen beim Universum*, translated into several languages and a German audio edition—which combined have more than half a million copies in print.

The author maintains a website, and the homepage, translated into English, can be accessed at www.baerbelmohr.de

Thank you for reading *The Cosmic Ordering Service*. Hampton Roads is proud to publish an extensive array of books on the topics discussed in this book, topics such as inspiration, personal transformation, and more. Visit us anytime on the web: www.hrpub.com.

Hampton Roads Publishing Company

. . . for the evolving human spirit

HAMPTON ROADS PUBLISHING COMPANY publishes books on a variety of subjects, including metaphysics, spirituality, health, visionary fiction, and other related topics.

For a copy of our latest trade catalog, call toll-free, 800-766-8009, or send your name and address to:

HAMPTON ROADS PUBLISHING COMPANY, INC.
1125 STONEY RIDGE ROAD • CHARLOTTESVILLE, VA 22902
e-mail: hrpc@hrpub.com • www.hrpub.com